# ARISTOTLE'S ETHICS
## (NICOMACHEAN)

*Aristotle*

© 2003 by Spark Publishing

SPARKNOTES is a registered trademark of SparkNotes LLC

Spark Publishing
A Division of Barnes & Noble
120 Fifth Avenue
New York, NY 10011
www.sparknotes.com

ISBN-13: 978-1-5866-3822-1
ISBN-10: 1-5866-3822-X

Please submit changes or report errors to www.sparknotes.com/errors.

Printed and bound in The United States.

5  7  9  10  8  6

# INTRODUCTION:
## STOPPING TO BUY SPARKNOTES ON A SNOWY EVENING

Whose words these are you *think* you know.
Your paper's due tomorrow, though;
We're glad to see you stopping here
To get some help before you go.

Lost your course? You'll find it here.
Face tests and essays without fear.
Between the words, good grades at stake:
Get great results throughout the year.

Once school bells caused your heart to quake
As teachers circled each mistake.
Use SparkNotes and no longer weep,
Ace every single test you take.

Yes, books are lovely, dark, and deep,
But only what you grasp you keep,
With hours to go before you sleep,
With hours to go before you sleep.

# CONTENTS

# CONTEXT

## BIOGRAPHICAL BACKGROUND

Aristotle was born at Stagira in northern Greece in 384 B.C. His father, Nicomachus, was a physician at the court of Philip of Macedon, the father of Alexander the Great. In 367, Aristotle moved to Athens, which was the intellectual and cultural center of ancient Greece. He spent many years studying in Plato's Academy, surrounded by other philosophers, scientists, and mathematicians. Plato died in 347, and Aristotle left the Academy in that same year. There is speculation that he left because Plato had not chosen him as his successor. It is more likely, however, that anti-Macedonian sentiment was growing in Athens, and Aristotle was afraid of being persecuted for his associations with King Philip's court.

Over the next four years, Aristotle traveled throughout the eastern Aegean area, studying and teaching. During this time, he conducted a remarkable array of experiments and observations in the biological sciences. In 343, he was summoned back north to Macedonia to be the personal tutor to the young Alexander the Great. While we know very little about Aristotle's influence on Alexander, there has been a great deal of speculation and mythologizing about the relationship between these two eminent figures.

As the Macedonians extended their empire over Greece, it became safe for Aristotle to return to Athens. In 334, he established his own philosophical school at the Lyceum, where he taught for the next eleven years. His lectures covered almost every area of study, including physics, metaphysics, ethics, psychology, politics, and poetry. His pioneering work in logic and biology was not improved upon for two thousand years.

In 323, Alexander the Great died, and Aristotle left Athens, fearing another upsurge of anti-Macedonian sentiment. Alluding to the trial and execution of Socrates some seventy-six years earlier, Aristotle reportedly claimed that he did not wish the Athenians to "sin a second time against philosophy." A year later, he died in Chalcis in Euboea.

Though Aristotle published many admired works in his lifetime, none have survived to the present day. Those works that we do have consist mostly of lecture notes from his courses at the Lyceum. That these works were never intended for publication explains why they are generally dry and hard to follow. The *Nicomachean Ethics* was likely either edited by or dedicated to Aristotle's son, Nicomachus.

## HISTORICAL CONTEXT

The Greek world of Aristotle's time was made up of small city-states, each with its own autonomous government. The city-state consisted of slaves, noncitizen manual laborers, children, women, aliens, and citizens. The citizens were adult males, most of whom had been born to citizen parents. The citizens governed the city, while the slaves, laborers, and women did all the work to provide the necessary food, shelter, and equipment. Because they were freed from the necessity of meeting day-to-day needs, citizens enjoyed a great deal of freedom and luxury. The leisure they enjoyed was highly valued and made possible one of the greatest periods of intellectual energy in human history. That this system was exploitative is hardly debatable, but it also produced an incredible array of philosophy, drama, art, and architecture. Aristotle's students were young citizens whose tuition was meant to prepare them for a life of civic duty.

There were few enough citizens that everyone in a given city would at least recognize, if not know, one another, and all citizens were expected to take part in public office. Unlike our modern system of representative democracy, where we simply elect officials to speak for us, all Greek citizens were expected to voice their own opinions in large deliberative and judicial assemblies. There was a strong bond of kinship created in citizenship, as the same people lived together, governed together, served in the army together, and enjoyed leisure time together.

The age of the city-state came to a close within Aristotle's lifetime, however, due to the efforts of his most famous pupil, Alexander the Great. Alexander came to power in the northern kingdom of Macedonia and within a decade had established one of the largest empires the world has ever seen. When Alexander died, Greece once more became fragmented, but the fierce independence of the city-states was a thing of the past. Greek culture was on the decline, and within a few hundred years, it would be swallowed up by the burgeoning Roman Empire.

## PHILOSOPHICAL CONTEXT

As the successor of Socrates and Plato, Aristotle was the last of the great Greek philosophers. Philosophy first flourished in Greece sometime in the early sixth century b.c. as inquisitive thinkers began developing rational methods for investigating the mysteries of nature and mathematics. These pre-Socratic thinkers were as much scientists and mathematicians as they were philosophers.

While there is significant pre-Socratic influence in Aristotle's work, primarily in the sciences and metaphysics, his most significant influence was undoubtedly Plato (427–347 B.C.). Plato's philosophy was centered on his famous Theory of Forms, or Theory of Ideas. The theory is based on the observation that there must be some universal quality that all things classed under a single name share in common. For instance, a flower is beautiful in a very different way from a human, but both the flower and the human must share something in common if we are to call them both "beautiful." Plato's answer is that they share in common the "Form of Beauty," which is itself invisible, unchanging, and eternal. Anything that we perceive in this world as beautiful is beautiful because it participates in some way in the Form of Beauty. But while beautiful flowers will wilt and beautiful humans will grow old and die, the Form of Beauty is everlasting and unchanging. Plato theorizes that our world of sensible experience, with its changes and disappointments, is but a poor reflection of the ideal world of pure Forms that underlies our experience. The goal of philosophy, then, is to train the mind to see beyond the veil of experience and to contemplate the true reality of Forms that lies behind it.

While Aristotle was undoubtedly influenced by Plato, this influence was mostly negative. Most of his works, including the *Nicomachean Ethics,* contain involved refutations of many of Plato's theories. Aristotle himself was an empirical scientist who felt that true wisdom comes from examining the objects of experience and not from trying to look beyond them. In the *Ethics,* he is primarily critical of Plato's Form of Good. According to Aristotle, there is not a single Form by virtue of which all good things are good. Instead, he discusses at length the multiplicity of the various virtues.

Aristotle's work in the *Ethics* is deeply informed by his own work in the sciences and metaphysics. Properly describing the breadth of Aristotle's impressive system is far beyond the scope of this Spark-

Note, but Jonathan Barnes's *Aristotle* (2000) provides an excellent and brief introduction to Aristotelian philosophy.

In terms of impact on the *Ethics,* perhaps Aristotle's most significant concept is that of the teleology of nature. According to Aristotle, nature works toward a *telos,* or end goal. His biological work aims constantly at the question of what purpose different aspects of plants and animals serve. He classifies humans as "rational animals," meaning that our *telos* is rational. In other words, our function in life is to realize our full potential as rational beings. If we are not fully rational, we are falling short of our true nature.

This teleological view gives Aristotle's *Ethics* a clear sense of direction. Our goal in life is to achieve our true nature, and this true nature consists essentially of rationality. The purpose of a moral education, then, is to teach us how we may become perfectly rational and immune to the temptations of our lower animalistic parts.

Ethics is just one of a number of fields that Aristotle classifies as "practical science." Unlike the natural sciences, which examine the world around us, these sciences deal with the practical aspects of human society and how best to arrange this society. The practical sciences are all closely connected, and Aristotle frequently expounds on the connection between the good life for the individual and the kind of state that could make this good life possible. Hence, Aristotle's *Politics* is an important companion and sequel to his *Ethics.*

While the *Nicomachean Ethics* is Aristotle's most popular work on ethics, there is a second work called the *Eudemian Ethics,* which is far less widely read. Most scholars agree that the *Eudemian Ethics* was written earlier in Aristotle's career and represents a less mature view. Books V, VI, and VII of the *Nicomachean Ethics* are also found in the *Eudemian Ethics.*

Aristotle's influence on Western philosophy is difficult to exaggerate. While his works were lost to the West for many centuries, they were slowly transmitted back into Europe by Arab scholars during the Middle Ages. Thanks mostly to the influence of Saint Thomas Aquinas, Aristotelian philosophy became accepted almost as dogmatically as the Bible during the late Middle Ages. While modern philosophy broke significantly from the scholastic tradition of the Middle Ages, Aristotle's influence remains undiminished. In particular, his emphasis on scientific reasoning and experimentation has been a cornerstone of modern empiricist philosophy.

# OVERVIEW

ALL HUMAN ACTIVITIES AIM AT SOME END that we consider good. Most activities are a means to a higher end. The highest human good, then, is that activity that is an end in itself. That good is happiness. When we aim at happiness, we do so for its own sake, not because happiness helps us realize some other end. The goal of the *Ethics* is to determine how best to achieve happiness. This study is necessarily imprecise, since so much depends on particular circumstances.

Happiness depends on living in accordance with appropriate virtues. Virtue is a disposition rather than an activity. That is, a virtuous person is naturally disposed to behave in the right ways and for the right reasons, and to feel pleasure in behaving rightly. Virtue is a mean state between the extremes of excess and deficiency. This mean varies from person to person, so there are no hard and fast rules as to how best to avoid vice.

Only voluntary actions are praiseworthy or blameworthy. We can define voluntary action as any action that originates in the agent and not in some outside force like a push or a stumble. There are borderline cases, however, as when someone is compelled to behave dishonorably under severe threat. Voluntary action is characterized by rational deliberation and choice, where the agent determines the best course of action by reasoning how best to achieve desirable ends.

One by one, Aristotle discusses the various moral virtues and their corresponding vices. Courage consists of confidence in the face of fear. Temperance consists of not giving in too easily to the pleasures of physical sensation. Liberality and magnificence consist of giving away varying amounts of money in appropriate and tasteful ways. Magnanimity and proper ambition consist of having the right disposition toward honor and knowing what is one's due. Patience is the appropriate disposition toward anger, though it is sometimes appropriate to show some degree of anger. The three social virtues of amiability, sincerity, and wit make for pleasant and engaging interaction with others. Modesty is not properly a virtue, but an appropriate disposition toward shame, which is admirable in the young.

Justice in a sense encompasses all the other virtues, since being just consists of exhibiting virtue generally. In human affairs, there are two primary forms of justice: distributive and rectificatory. Distributive justice deals with the distribution of wealth or honors among a group of people and should be given according to merit. Rectificatory justice deals with exchanges between two or more people and should always aim at restoring a sense of balance and equality between the people concerned. It is impossible to treat oneself unjustly or to suffer injustice willingly. While the laws are a good guideline, they do not cover every particular case. On occasion, agreed-upon equity must settle cases that the laws do not.

While the moral virtues dispose us to behave in the correct manner, it is necessary also to have the right intellectual virtues in order to reason properly about how to behave. There are five intellectual virtues. Three of them—scientific knowledge, intuition, and wisdom—consist of contemplative reasoning, which is detached from human affairs. The other two—art or technical skill and prudence—consist of calculative reasoning, which helps us make our way in the world. Prudence is the intellectual virtue that helps us reason properly about ethical matters.

Incontinence is a peculiar form of badness. Unlike vice, incontinence does not involve willing bad behavior. Rather, it consists of knowing what is good but lacking the self-control to do good. Incontinence is not as bad as vice, since it is partially involuntary.

There are three kinds of friendship: friendship based on utility, friendship based on pleasure, and friendship based on goodness of character. The first two kinds of friendship are based on superficial qualities, so these sorts of friendship are not generally long lasting. Friendship based on goodness of character is the best kind of friendship, because these friends love one another for who they are and not for what they stand to gain from one another. Friendship generally exists between equals, though there are cases, like the father-son relationship, which rely on unequal exchanges.

Political institutions rely on friendly feelings between citizens, so friendship and justice are closely connected. There are three forms of constitution based on different kinds of relationships. Of the three, monarchy is preferable to aristocracy or timocracy.

Ideally, our feelings for our friends should reflect our feelings for ourselves. Self-love is more important than friendship, since only people who treat themselves with appropriate care and respect can achieve proper virtue and happiness. Though a happy person is theoretically self-sufficient, friendship is an important and essential aspect of the good life.

Pleasure accompanies and perfects our activities. A good person will feel pleasure in doing good things. The highest good of all is rational contemplation. A life that consists exclusively of contemplation is obviously impossible, but we should aim to approximate this ideal as closely as possible. The practical sciences, then, help us find the right path toward this highest good and help us deal with the practical matters of everyday life that inevitably occupy a great deal of our time and attention.

# TERMS

*Akrasia*   Usually translated as "incontinence," this term
connotes a lack of self-control. A person exhibiting
*akrasia* knows what good behavior consists of but
lacks the self-control not to give in to physical
pleasures. The concept of *akrasia* is significant to
Aristotle, as he generally agrees with the Socratic claim
that no one willingly does evil and that all wrongdoing
is a result of ignorance. If the incontinent person acts
wrongly in full knowledge of what is good, this poses a
dilemma for Socratic ethics, which Book VII of the
*Ethics* attempts to answer.

*Arete*   Usually translated as "virtue," this important term
means something more akin to "excellence." For the
Greeks, *arete* can be used to refer not only to a person's
moral or intellectual virtues, but to any other kind of
excellence, be it the fitness of an athlete or even the
sharpness of a knife. Generally speaking, a person,
animal, or thing exhibits *arete* when it is performing its
function properly. That the Greeks use the term *arete* in
their discussions of ethics implies a strong sense that
humans have a function just as knives do, and that we
become good by fulfilling this function.

*Doctrine of the Mean*   Aristotle's doctrine, stated most explicitly
in Book II, that virtue is a mean state between the
vicious extremes of excess and deficiency. This doctrine
is left necessarily vague, as Aristotle thinks that this
mean varies from person to person. Essentially, it
consists of the observation that it is always possible to
have too much or too little of a good thing.

*Energeia*   This Greek word, which is the root of our word *energy,*
is generally translated as "activity." However, it is not
necessarily an activity in the sense that we might
understand it. For instance, Aristotle describes both
happiness and contemplation as activities. In calling

9

happiness an *energeia,* Aristotle contrasts it with virtue, which he considers to be a *hexis,* or disposition. That is, the virtues dispose us to behave in the correct manner. Actually behaving according to the virtues, however, is not itself a virtue but rather the *energeia* of happiness.

*Ethos*   We can see that this term is the root of our word *ethics.* However, it is more accurately translated as "character," which gives us an important insight to understanding the *Ethics.* Aristotle is not so much concerned with moralizing as he is with determining what constitutes an admirable character.

*Eudaimonia*   Normally translated as "happiness," *eudaimonia* also carries connotations of success and fulfillment. For the Greeks, happiness is not an inner, emotional state, but the activity, or *energeia,* of a successful person. The Greeks did not share our sharp distinction between the public and the private, so for them, happiness is a public matter that can be evaluated just as accurately by an observer as by the person being observed.

*Hexis*   Translated as "disposition," *hexis* is the term Aristotle uses to qualify the virtues. According to Aristotle, virtue is not something one actively does. Rather, virtue is a disposition to behave in the right way.

*Phronesis*   Often translated as "prudence," this term is perhaps better, but more cumbersomely, translated as "practical wisdom." *Phronesis* is an important intellectual virtue that allows us to reason properly about practical matters. *Phronesis* consists in no small part of an appropriate application of the practical syllogism.

*Practical syllogism*   A syllogism is a three-term argument consisting of a major premise stating some universal truth (e.g., "All horses have four legs"), a minor premise stating some particular truth (e.g., "Black Beauty is a horse"), and a conclusion derived from these two premises (e.g., "Therefore, Black Beauty has four legs"). The practical syllogism is a form of practical reasoning in syllogistic form, the conclusion of which is an action. An example might be that the major premise "All intruders will be shot on sight" and the minor premise "I see an intruder over there" leads to the practical conclusion of shooting at the intruder.

*Psuche*     The root of our word *psychology, psuche* is generally translated as "soul," though it carries none of the spiritual connotations of the Christian use of that word. *Psuche* is that unobservable property that distinguishes living things from nonliving things. The human *psuche* consists of three major parts: the nutritive part, which it shares with both plants and animals; the appetitive part, which it shares with only animals; and the rational part, which is distinctively human.

*Telos*     This important term can be translated variously as "end," "goal," or "purpose." According to Aristotle, we have a *telos* as humans, which it is our goal to fulfill. This *telos* is based on our uniquely human capacity for rational thought. Aristotle's view of humans having a *telos* based in our rationality leads directly to his conclusion in Book X that contemplation is the highest human good.

TERMS

# VIRTUES AND VICES

| SPHERE OF ACTION OF FEELING | EXCESS | MEAN | DEFICIENCY |
|---|---|---|---|
| Fear and Confidence | Rashness | Courage | Cowardice |
| Pleasure and Pain | Licentiousness | Temperance | Insensibility |
| Getting and Spending (minor) | Prodigality | Liberality | Illiberality |
| Getting and Spending (major) | Vulgarity | Magnificence | Pettiness |
| Honor and Dishonor (minor) | Ambition | Proper Ambition | Unambitiousness |
| Honor and Dishonor (major) | Vanity | Magnanimity | Pusillanimity |
| Anger | Irascibility | Patience | Lack of Spirit |
| Self-expression | Boastfulness | Truthfulness | Understatement |
| Conversation | Buffoonery | Wittiness | Boorishness |
| Social Conduct | Obsequiousness or Flattery | Friendliness | Cantankerousness |
| Shame | Shyness | Modesty | Shamelessness |
| Indignation | Envy | Righteous indignation | Malicious enjoyment |

TERMS

# THEMES, IDEAS & ARGUMENTS

## VIRTUE AND HAPPINESS

The word *happiness* in the *Ethics* is a translation of the Greek term *eudaimonia,* which carries connotations of success and fulfillment. For Aristotle, this happiness is our highest goal. However, Aristotle does not say that we *should* aim at happiness, but rather that we *do* aim at happiness. His goal in the *Ethics* is not to tell us that we ought to live happy, successful lives, but to tell us what this life consists of. Most people think of happiness as physical pleasure or honor, but this is because they have an imperfect view of the good life.

The conception people have of happiness frequently does not line up with true happiness because people are generally deficient in virtue. Virtue is a disposition to behave in the right manner, which is inculcated from a young age. A person with the virtue of courage, for instance, will not only show confidence in the face of fear, but will think of this courage as a good thing. Behaving courageously will make the virtuous person happy and will be one part of living a generally good life. By contrast, a person who has been poorly brought up and exhibits the vice of cowardice will find happiness in the avoidance of danger and thus will have an imperfect view of the good life.

## MORAL EDUCATION

A question of high importance in any investigation of ethics is how we can teach people to be good. Aristotle is quite clear that he does not think virtue can be taught in a classroom or by means of argument. His *Ethics,* then, is not designed to make people good, but rather to explain what is good, why it is good, and how we might set about building societies and institutions that might inculcate this goodness.

According to Aristotle, virtue is something learned through constant practice that begins at a young age. We might understand his outlook better if we recognize the meaning of the word *arete,* which is rendered as "virtue" in most English translations. This term more generally means "excellence," so a good horseman can exhibit *arete* in horsemanship without necessarily implying any sort of moral worth in the horseman. It should be obvious to anyone that excellence in horsemanship cannot be learned simply by reading about horsemanship and hearing reasoned arguments for how best to handle a horse. Becoming a good horseman requires steady practice: one learns to handle a horse by spending a lot of time riding horses.

For Aristotle, there is no essential distinction between the kind of excellence that marks a good horseman and the kind of excellence that marks a good person generally. Both kinds of excellence require practice first and theoretical study second, so the teaching of virtue can be only of secondary importance after the actual practice of it.

## THE DOCTRINE OF THE MEAN

One of the most famous aspects of the *Ethics* is Aristotle's doctrine that virtue exists as a mean state between the vicious extremes of excess and deficiency. For example, the virtuous mean of courage stands between the vices of rashness and cowardice, which represent excess and deficiency respectively.

For Aristotle, this is not a precise formulation. Saying that courage is a mean between rashness and cowardice does not mean that courage stands exactly in between these two extremes, nor does it mean that courage is the same for all people. Aristotle repeatedly reminds us in the *Ethics* that there are no general laws or exact formulations in the practical sciences. Rather, we need to approach matters case by case, informed by inculcated virtue and a fair dose of practical wisdom.

Aristotle's claim that virtue can be learned only through constant practice implies that there are no set rules we can learn and then obey. Instead, virtue consists of learning through experience what is the mean path, relative to ourselves, between the vices we may be liable to stumble into.

## THE UNITY OF THE VIRTUES

For Aristotle, virtue is an all-or-nothing affair. We cannot pick and choose our virtues: we cannot decide that we will be courageous and temperate but choose not to be magnificent. Nor can we call people properly virtuous if they fail to exhibit all of the virtues.

Though Aristotle lists a number of virtues, he sees them all as coming from the same source. A virtuous person is someone who is naturally disposed to exhibit all the virtues, and a naturally virtuous disposition exhibits all the virtues equally.

Our word *ethics* descends from the Greek word *ethos,* which means more properly "character." Aristotle's concern in the *Ethics,* then, is what constitutes a good character. All the virtues spring from a unified character, so no good person can exhibit some virtues without exhibiting them all.

## THE IMPORTANCE OF FRIENDSHIP

Aristotle devotes two of the ten books of the *Ethics* to discussing friendship in all its forms. This is hardly a digression from the main line of argument. Happiness, according to Aristotle, is a public affair, not a private one, so with whom we share this happiness is of great significance.

The city-states of ancient Greece were tightly knit communities. In the *Politics,* Aristotle argues that we cannot fully realize our human nature outside the bounds of a Greek city-state. The bonds that tie citizens together are so important that it would be unthinkable to suggest that true happiness can be found in the life of a hermit.

## THE LIFE OF CONTEMPLATION

In Book X, Aristotle ultimately concludes that contemplation is the highest human activity. This is largely a consequence of his teleological view of nature, according to which the *telos,* or goal, of human life is the exercise of our rational powers. In discussing the various intellectual virtues, Aristotle extols wisdom as the highest, since it deals only with unchanging, universal truths and rests on a synthesis of scientific investigation and the intuitive understanding of the first principles of nature. The activity of wisdom is contemplation, so contemplation must be the highest activity of human life.

THEMES, IDEAS, ARGUMENTS

# Summary & Analysis

## Book I

### Summary

> Our account of this science will be adequate if it
> achieves such clarity as the subject matter allows.
>
> *(See* QUOTATIONS, *p. 51)*

Every human activity aims at some end that we consider good. The highest ends are ends in themselves, while subordinate ends may only be means to higher ends. Those highest ends, which we pursue for their own sake, must be the supreme Good.

The study of the Good is part of political science, because politics concerns itself with securing the highest ends for human life. Politics is not a precise science, since what is best for one person may not be best for another. Consequently, we can aim at only a rough outline of the Good.

Everyone agrees that the supreme Good is happiness, but people disagree over what constitutes happiness. Common people equate happiness with sensual pleasure: this may be sufficient for animals, but human life has higher ends. Others say that receiving honors is the greatest good, but honors are conferred as recognition of goodness, so there must be a greater good that these honors reward. Plato's Theory of Forms suggests that there is a single Form of Good and that all good things are good in the same way. This theory seems flawed when we consider the diversity of things we call "good" and the diversity of ways in which we consider goodness. Even if there were a single unifying Form of Good, our interest is in the practical question of how to be good, so we should concern ourselves not with this abstract concept but with the practical ends we can actually pursue in everyday life.

Happiness is the highest good because we choose happiness as an end sufficient in itself. Even intelligence and virtue are not good only in themselves, but good also because they make us happy.

We call people "good" if they perform their function well. For instance, a person who plays the flute well is a good flutist. Playing the flute is the flutist's function because that is his or her distinctive activity. The distinctive activity of humans generally—what distinguishes us from plants and animals—is our rationality. Therefore, the supreme Good should be an activity of the rational soul in accordance with virtue. This definition aligns with popular views of happiness, which see the happy person as virtuous, rational, and active.

When talking about happiness, we consider a person's life as a whole, not just brief moments of it. This raises the paradoxical suggestion that a person can be considered happy only after death, that is, once we can examine the person's life as a whole. However, a good person will always behave in a virtuous manner. Even faced with great misfortune, a good person will bear himself or herself well and will not descend into mean-spiritedness. Once a person has died, according to Aristotle, posthumous honors or dishonors and the behavior of his descendants might affect his happiness somewhat, but to no great extent.

We can divide the soul into an irrational and a rational part. The irrational soul has two aspects: the vegetative aspect, which deals with nutrition and growth and has little connection to virtue; and the appetitive aspect, which governs our impulses. The rational part of the soul controls these impulses, so a virtuous person with greater rationality is better able to control his or her impulses.

## ANALYSIS

Much confusion about Aristotle's work comes not from Aristotle's lack of clarity, but from an imprecision in translation. Ancient Greek is quite different from the English language, and more important, the ancient Greeks lived in a very different culture that used concepts for which there are no exact English translations.

One central concept of the *Ethics* is *eudaimonia,* which is generally translated as "happiness." While happiness is probably the best English word to translate *eudaimonia,* the term also carries connotations of success, fulfillment, and flourishing. A person who is *eudaimon* is not simply enjoying life, but is enjoying life by living successfully. One's success and reputation, unlike one's emotional well-being, can be affected after death, which makes Aristotle's discussion of *eudaimonia* after death considerably more relevant.

That happiness should be closely connected to success and fulfillment reflects an important aspect of social life in ancient Greece. The identity of Greek citizens was so closely linked to the city-state to which they belonged that exile was often thought of as a fate worse than death. There was no distinction between the public and private spheres as exists in the modern world. Consequently, happiness was not thought of as a private affair, dependent on individual emotional states, but as a reflection of a person's position within a city-state. A person who inhabits a proper place in the social structure and who appropriately fulfills the duties and expectations of that place is "happy" because, for the Greeks, happiness is a matter of living—not just feeling—the right way.

Aristotle treats happiness as an activity, not as a state. He uses the word *energeia*, which is the root of our word *energy*, to characterize happiness. The point is that happiness consists of a certain way of life, not of certain dispositions. In saying that happiness is an *energeia*, he contrasts happiness with virtue, which he considers a *hexis*, or state of being. Possessing all the right virtues disposes a person to live well, while happiness is the activity of living well, which the virtuous person is inclined toward.

> [T]he good for man is an activity of the soul in
> accordance with virtue, or if there are more kinds of
> virtue than one, in accordance with the best and most
> perfect kind.
>
> (See QUOTATIONS, p. 52)

The very idea of living well might seem a bit odd as Aristotle formulates it. In particular, he talks about living well as performing the function of "being human" well, analogous to the good flutist performing the function of playing the flute well. It may seem that Aristotle has confused the practical and the moral: being a good flutist is a practical matter of study and talent, while no such analogy holds for morality. Being a good person surely is not a skill one develops in the same manner as flute playing. But this objection rests on a misunderstanding due to a difficulty in translation. The Greek word *ethos* translates as "character," and the concerns of the *Ethics* are not with determining what is right and wrong, but with how to live a virtuous and happy life.

We should also note the importance of the concept of *telos*, which we might translate as "end" or "goal." The first sentence of the *Ethics* tells us that every activity aims at a certain *telos*. For instance, one might go to the gym with the *telos* of becoming fitter. When Aristotle identifies happiness as the highest goal, he is claiming that happiness is the ultimate *telos* of any action. We might understand this idea of an ultimate *telos* by imagining the child who constantly asks, "why?":

SUMMARY & ANALYSIS

"Why are you going to the gym?"

"To become fitter."

"Why do you want to become fitter?"

"So that I'll be healthier."

"Why do you want to be healthy?"

"So that I'll live longer and have more energy."

"Why do you want a long and energetic life?"

"Because that makes for a happy life."

"Why do you want a happy life?"

"I just do."

Every activity has a *telos,* which is an answer to the question, *Why are you doing this?* Happiness is the ultimate *telos* because there is no further *telos* beyond happiness and because the ultimate goal of all our other activities is happiness.

For Aristotle, the soul, or *psuche* (the root of our word *psychology*), is simply that which distinguishes living things from nonliving things. All living things have a nutritive soul, which governs bodily health and growth. Animals and humans differ from plants in having an appetitive soul, which governs movement and impulse. Humans differ from animals in also having a rational soul, which governs thought and reason. Because rationality is the unique achievement of humans, Aristotle sees rationality as our *telos*: in his view, everything exists for a purpose, and the purpose of human life is to develop and exercise our rational soul. Consequently, a human can "be human" well by developing reason in the way that a flutist can be a good flutist by developing skill with the flute.

# Book II

> *So virtue is a purposive disposition, lying in a mean that is relative to us and determined by a rational principle, by that which a prudent man would use to determine it.*
>
> (See QUOTATIONS, p. 53)

## Summary

There are two kinds of virtue: intellectual and moral. We learn intellectual virtues by instruction, and we learn moral virtues by habit and constant practice. We are all born with the potential to be morally virtuous, but it is only by behaving in the right way that we train ourselves to be virtuous. As a musician learns to play an instrument, we learn virtue by practicing, not by thinking about it.

Because practical circumstances vary a great deal, there are no absolute rules of conduct to follow. Instead, we can only observe that right conduct consists of some sort of mean between the extremes of deficiency and excess. For instance, courage consists in finding a mean between the extremes of cowardice and rashness, though the appropriate amount of courage varies from one situation to another.

An appropriate attitude toward pleasure and pain is one of the most important habits to develop for moral virtue. While a glutton might feel inappropriate pleasure when presented with food and inappropriate pain when deprived of food, a temperate person will gain pleasure from abstaining from such indulgence.

Aristotle proposes three criteria to distinguish virtuous people from people who behave in the right way by accident: first, virtuous people know they are behaving in the right way; second, they choose to behave in the right way for the sake of being virtuous; and third, their behavior manifests itself as part of a fixed, virtuous disposition.

Virtue is a disposition, not a feeling or a faculty. Feelings are not the subject of praise or blame, as virtues and vices are, and while feelings move us to act in a certain way, virtues dispose us to act in a certain way. Our faculties determine our capacity for feelings, and virtue is no more a capacity for feeling than it is a feeling itself. Rather, it is a disposition to behave in the right way.

We can now define human virtue as a disposition to behave in the right manner and as a mean between extremes of deficiency and excess, which are vices. Of course, with some actions, such as murder or adultery, there is no virtuous mean, since these actions are always wrong. Aristotle lists some of the principle virtues along with their corresponding vices of excess and deficiency in a table of virtues and vices. Some extremes seem closer to the mean than others: for instance, rashness seems closer to courage than to cowardice. This is partly because courage is more like rashness than cowardice and partly because most of us are more inclined to be cowardly than rash, so we are more aware of being deficient in courage.

Aristotle suggests three practical rules of conduct: first, avoid the extreme that is farther from the mean; second, notice what errors we are particularly susceptible to and avoid them diligently; and third, be wary of pleasure, as it often impedes our judgment.

## ANALYSIS

"Virtue" is the most common translation of the Greek word *arete,* though it is occasionally translated as "excellence." Virtue is usually an adequate translation in the *Ethics* because it deals specifically with human excellence, but *arete* could be used to describe any kind of excellence, such as the sharpness of a knife or the fitness of an athlete. Just as a knife's excellence rests in its sharpness, a person's excellence rests in living according to the various moral and intellectual virtues.

Aristotle describes virtue as a disposition, distinguishing it not only from feelings and faculties, but also (less explicitly) from activities. Aristotle calls happiness an activity, or *energeia,* in Book I, meaning that happiness is not an emotional state but a way of life. Happiness is exhibited not in how we are but in how we act. Virtue, by contrast, is a disposition, or *hexis,* meaning that it is a state of being and not an activity. More precisely, virtue is the disposition to act in such a way as to lead a happy life.

Without virtue, we cannot be happy, though possessing virtue does not in itself guarantee happiness. In Book I, Chapter 8, Aristotle points out that those who win honors at the Olympic Games are not necessarily the strongest people present but rather the strongest people who actually compete. Perhaps one of the spectators is stronger than all of the competitors, but this spectator has no right to win honors. Similarly, a person might have a virtuous disposition but will not lead a happy life unless he or she acts according to this disposition.

It may seem odd to us that Aristotle at no point argues for what dispositions should be considered virtuous and which vicious. The need for justification seems even more pressing in the modern world, where our views on virtue and vice may not entirely agree with Aristotle's.

However, it is not Aristotle's intention to convince us of what is virtuous, and he differs from most modern moral philosophers in placing very little emphasis on rational argument in moral development. Instead, as he argues at the beginning of Book II, learning virtue is a matter of habit and proper training. We do not become courageous by learning why courage is preferable to cowardice or rashness, but rather by being trained to be courageous. Only when we have learned to be instinctively courageous can we rightly arrive at any reasoned approval of courage. Recalling that *arete* may refer to any form of excellence, we might draw an analogy between learning courage and learning rock-climbing. We learn to become good rock-climbers through constant practice, not through reasoned arguments, and only when we have become good rock-climbers and appreciate firsthand the joys of rock-climbing can we properly understand why rock-climbing is a worthwhile activity.

Aristotle's conception of virtue as something learned through habit rather than through reasoning makes a great deal of practical sense. We can generally trace unpleasantness to the circumstances in which a person grew up, and it is difficult to make an unpleasant person pleasant simply by providing reasons for behaving more pleasantly.

The virtues Aristotle lists, then, reflect the commonly held values of a properly raised, aristocratic Athenian. If we disagree with Aristotle's choices of virtues, we are unlikely to find a compelling argument in his work to change our mind: by Aristotle's own admission, reasoning is unlikely to teach us to appreciate virtue if we have not been raised with the right habits.

One of the most celebrated and discussed aspects of Aristotle's *Ethics* is his Doctrine of the Mean, which holds that every virtue is a mean between the vicious extremes of excess and deficiency. This is not a strict rule, as Aristotle himself points out: there is no precise formula by which we can determine exactly where this mean lies, largely because the mean will vary for different people.

That there should be no fixed rule to determine where the mean lies is a direct consequence of his doctrine that virtue is something learned through habit, not through reason. If we could reason our way into virtue, we might be able to set out precise rules for how to behave in different situations. According to Aristotle's view, however, a virtuous person is naturally inclined to choose the correct behavior in any situation without appealing to rules or maxims.

In Book I, Chapter 3, and Book II, Chapter 2, Aristotle warns us that our inquiry is at best an imprecise one. Bearing in mind that virtue for Aristotle is a set of innate dispositions, not a reasoned set of rules, we can understand these warnings to be more than simple hedges. Aristotle is not avoiding precision but saying that precision is impossible because there are no fixed rules of conduct that we can follow with confidence.

# Book III

## Summary

Our evaluation of a person's actions depends to some extent on whether those actions are voluntary, involuntary, or nonvoluntary. An action is involuntary when it is performed under compulsion and causes pain to the person acting. There are borderline cases, as when someone is compelled to do something dishonorable under threat, but we should generally consider such cases voluntary, since the person is still in control of his or her actions. Something done in ignorance may be called involuntary if the person later recognizes that ignorance, but it is nonvoluntary if the person does not recognize or suffer for such ignorance. However, ignorance can excuse only particular cases, and not general behavior, since general ignorance of what is good is precisely what makes a person bad.

It seems the best measure of moral goodness is choice, because unlike actions, choices are always made voluntarily. We make choices about the means we use to achieve a desired end. Deliberation, which precedes choice, is directed only toward those means over which we have some control and only when the correct manner of proceeding is not immediately obvious.

Deliberation proceeds according to the analytical method. We consider first what end we wish to achieve, and then reason backward to the means we might implement to bring about this end.

In choosing, those of good character will always aim for the good. However, those who are not of good character may understand things incorrectly and may wish for only the *apparent* good. Both virtue and vice, therefore, lie within human power, because they are related to choices that we make voluntarily and deliberately. This conclusion is borne out by the fact that rewards and punishments are only conferred on those actions that we are thought to have done voluntarily. People who behave badly form bad habits that are difficult to change, but their lack of self-control is hardly an excuse for their badness.

Having examined virtue in the abstract, Aristotle examines each particular virtue, starting with courage, which he defines as the appropriate attitude toward fear. Courage does not mean fearlessness, as there are some things, such as shame or brutality toward one's family, which one ought to fear. Rather, courage involves confidence in the face of fear, best exhibited on the battlefield, where men show themselves unafraid to die an honorable death. An excess of fearfulness constitutes the vice of cowardice, and a deficiency constitutes rashness.

Certain dispositions resemble courage but are not in fact courageous. The soldier who fights for fear of dishonor, the veteran who shows no fear in the face of what he knows to be a false alarm, the spirited soldier aroused by anger or pain, the sanguine man who is unafraid due to overconfidence, and the soldier ignorant of the dan-

SUMMARY & ANALYSIS

ger he faces are not courageous. Courage is a difficult and admirable virtue, because it involves enduring pain.

Temperance is the mean state with regard to physical pleasure, while licentiousness is the vice of excessive yearning for physical pleasure. The grossest pleasures are those of taste, and especially touch, which are most liable to be sources of licentiousness. The licentious person feels not only excessive pleasure with regard to physical sensations, but also excessive pain when deprived of these pleasures. The vice of deficiency toward pleasure is so rare that it lacks a name, though we could perhaps call it insensibility. The temperate person will feel appropriate amounts of pleasure, and only toward those things that are conducive to health and fitness.

## ANALYSIS

The problem of free will is much debated in modern moral philosophy. Presumably, we can be held morally responsible only for those actions that we perform of our own free will, so determining the source and scope of our freedom would seem a necessary prerequisite to determining the source and scope of moral responsibility. Discussing free will raises a number of metaphysical problems, however, foremost of which is the problem of determinism. If we are subject to predictable and unchanging physical laws, then we have no freedom to do what we want. Some philosophers argue that free will is an illusion, some argue that determinism is an illusion, and some argue that a proper understanding of the concepts of free will and determinism will show that the two concepts are in fact compatible.

Aristotle seems strangely unconcerned with the metaphysical vagaries of free will. He makes no mention of the concept of free will, thus avoiding the metaphysical question of whether free will can be compatible with determinism. Furthermore, he seems to avoid any strict definition of responsible action that might delimit for us precisely what kinds of actions we should be held responsible for. At best, he gives us a negative definition, telling us that we are not responsible for actions done under ignorance or compulsion.

However, Aristotle adds some caveats. Ignorance is only an acceptable excuse if we are not responsible for our ignorance. Aristotle seems to agree with Socrates' claim that no one knowingly does evil and that all wrongdoing is a result of ignorance. He suggests in Chapter 4 of Book III that everyone aims to do good, but bad people, in their ignorance, aim at the *apparent* good that is in fact not good.

The question, then, is to what extent we can be held responsible for our ignorance. Aristotle's answer seems to be that the ignorance must be related to particular circumstances over which the agent had no control. For instance, a man is not responsible for poisoning a friend if he had no way of knowing that the drink he gave this friend was poisoned. However, a man who lacks a proper sense of virtue and who does a bad deed through ignorance of what is good is certainly responsible for his badness.

Aristotle similarly explains compulsion. He takes a particularly stern stance on the question of what sorts of compulsion render an act involuntary: involuntary acts are only those that do not originate with the agent. For instance, if someone pushes me into you, I have bumped you involuntarily, because my sudden movement did not originate with me.

Aristotle then implies that unpleasant decisions made under threats or danger are voluntary, though he offers some leniency to those who make the best choice from a series of unenviable options.

In defining those cases of exemption from moral responsibility due to ignorance or compulsion, however, Aristotle does not provide a positive definition of moral responsibility, and he certainly does not give us a definition of free will. The most plausible explanation for this seeming omission is that Aristotle's interest does not lie in the metaphysics of moral responsibility. His only interest is the juridical question of where we can assign praise or blame.

Nonetheless, Aristotle does rely on many of the same tenets of modern ethical theory, such as the importance of choice and deliberation. Aristotle argues that we are not primarily responsible for the results of our choices, but for the choices themselves. That is why, for instance, the well-wishing man who inadvertently poisons his friend is not to be condemned: he made the right choice, and the unfortunate result was due to unavoidable ignorance on his part.

However, this emphasis on choice seems to conflict somewhat with what Aristotle says about virtue. In Book II, he distinguishes the person who accidentally exhibits courage from the truly courageous person by saying that the virtuous man sees courage as an end in itself. In this case, the choice and the action are the same: the courageous man chooses to be courageous for the sake of being courageous.

But now Aristotle tells us that choices are virtuous because of the noble ends at which they aim. A soldier who fights through an enemy file to relieve his embattled friends is presumably courageous and hence virtuous because he made a choice to relieve his friends and followed through with this choice in spite of the fear he faced in doing so. Surely, the end goal this soldier had in mind, the goal that led him to choose to fight through the enemy file, was to relieve his friends. But this scenario conflicts with Aristotle's suggestion that the courageous person sees courage as an end in itself and pursues it as such.

# Book IV

## Summary

Having discussed courage and temperance in Book III, Aristotle now moves through the rest of the virtues, discussing them one by one.

Liberality is the right disposition with regard to spending money, while prodigality and illiberality represent excess and deficiency respectively. The liberal person will give the right amounts of money to the right people at the right times and so will take pleasure in giving: giving money only grudgingly is a sign of illiberality. Feeling no strong attachment to money, the liberal person manages resources well and does not squander money as the prodigal person would. Prodigality is better than illiberality because it is a result of foolishness rather than vice and can be easily remedied.

While liberality deals with ordinary expenditures of money, magnificence is the virtue of properly spending large sums of money on liturgies, or public gifts. Magnificence requires good taste: gaudy displays of wealth exhibit the vice of vulgarity, while spoiling a liturgy through penny-pinching is a sign of pettiness.

Magnanimity is the quality of the person who knows himself or herself to be worthy of great honors. The person who overestimates self-worth is conceited, and the person who underestimates self-worth is pusillanimous. Neither vanity nor pusillanimity are so much bad as mistaken, though pusillanimity is generally worse. The magnanimous person is great and knows it. This person therefore accepts honors knowing they are deserved, but does not take excessive pleasure in these honors. Being aware of his or her greatness and status, the magnanimous person is uncomfortable when put in a position inferior to anyone and always seeks his or her rightful superior place. Aristotle asserts of the magnanimous person that "his gait is measured, his voice deep, and his speech unhurried."

With regard to smaller honors, there is a virtuous mean, which lies between the excess of extreme ambition and the deficiency of lacking ambition entirely.

The right disposition toward anger is similar to patience, though patience can sometimes be a deficiency, as some anger is occasionally appropriate. The excess of irascibility manifests itself in people with hot tempers, or worse, people who hold grudges and remain irritable.

Amiability, sincerity, and wit are important social virtues. Amiability is the virtuous quality of appropriate social conduct. An overeagerness to please exhibits itself in obsequiousness or flattery, while surly or quarrelsome behavior exhibits a deficiency of amiability.

Truthfulness or sincerity is a desirable mean state between the deficiency of irony or self-deprecation and the excess of boastfulness. Self-deprecation is acceptable unless it is overly pretentious, and it is certainly preferable to boastfulness, which is especially blameworthy when the boasting is directed at making undeserved gains.

Wit is important to good conversation. A person lacking in wit is boorish and will be uninteresting and easily offended. By contrast, buffoonery is the excessive vice of being too eager to get a laugh: tact is an important component of appropriate wit.

Modesty is not properly a virtue but rather a feeling that a well-bred youth ought to be capable of. Modesty consists of feeling shame at the appropriate times. A virtuous person will never do anything shameful and so will have no need of modesty, but a youth will learn to be virtuous only by feeling shame when shame is called for.

---

## ANALYSIS

Aristotle focuses on details in his discussion of the various virtues and vices. He discusses questions such as which vicious extreme is worse than the other and whether a particular vice is truly evil or simply a result of folly or ignorance. By contrast, we find no general attempt at justifying Aristotle's choices of virtues and vices. The absence of general justification is made particularly glaring by the 2,300-year gap between Aristotle and ourselves. While the modern West takes some influence from the ancient Greeks, our conceptions of virtue and vice are certainly more informed by the Christian tradition than by the Greek. Aristotle makes no mention of the Christian virtues of charity, faith, or hope, and the Christian virtue of humility is considered by Aristotle to be a vice: pusillanimity.

Aristotle provides no argument for his list of virtues and vices because he assumes his readers will agree with his conception. In Book II, he asserts that virtue can be learned only through practice: no set of rational arguments can make a person virtuous.

In simply assuming a set of virtues, Aristotle may not be as far from modern moral philosophers as we think. Immanuel Kant is unlike Aristotle in that he tries to build a rational foundation for his moral maxims, but the maxims he arrives at, such as "never tell a lie under any circumstances," are maxims we might expect from a man who was raised in a strictly Lutheran family. We might argue that Kant develops arguments that justify his preheld moral beliefs rather than approaching his conclusions with an open mind.

No one can build a moral theory from the ground up, because everyone starts with some set of moral assumptions. Philosophical theorizing might lead us to revise some of our earlier moral assumptions, but it cannot proceed without acknowledging that some moral assumptions are already in place. Similarly with Aristotle: he critically examines various virtues and vices, determining, for instance, that modesty is not in fact a virtue, but he does so only after acknowledging the moral assumptions he starts with. Moral reasoning would be impossible without some prior conception of morality.

Of course, this brings us no closer to answering the question of what we are to make of Aristotle's virtues and vices if we do not agree with them. Aristotle provides us with no compelling reasons to change our minds. We might further ask how seriously we can take Aristotle's *Ethics* as a whole if we do not accept some of his virtues and vices.

There is no easy answer to these questions. Surely Aristotle's project is not endangered as a whole if we reject his condemnation of humility, but there is some question as to how seriously we can take Aristotle's description of the good life if we do not think of the life he describes as particularly good. Perhaps the best way to begin approaching the problem is to understand the way of life that Aristotle's virtues represent.

Aristotle tells us that we cannot take the virtues piecemeal: we cannot consider a person to be truly virtuous unless that person possesses all the virtues. Two of the virtues, magnificence and magnanimity, apply only to people of considerable wealth and honor. This leads us to the uncomfortable conclusion that only wealthy people can be truly virtuous.

This conclusion would not have been uncomfortable for Aristotle: he was a member of the aristocratic class and lectured only to fellow aristocrats, all of whom would have agreed that only they, as aristocrats, could be truly virtuous. In his *Politics*, Aristotle argues that only the independently wealthy can fully enjoy the good life.

There is an obvious class bias in Aristotle's arguments. However, we should remember that he does not distinguish sharply between moral success and happy living. It is obvious that Aristotle and his fellow aristocrats enjoyed a much higher standard of living than the working class, women, and slaves, and that they could lay claim to greater happiness. This high standard of living makes true success and happiness, or *eudaimonia,* possible, so only this high standard of living can be an adequate expression of all the virtues.

# BOOK V

## SUMMARY

Justice can mean either lawfulness or fairness, since injustice is lawlessness and unfairness. The laws encourage people to behave virtuously, so the just person, who by definition is lawful, will necessarily be virtuous. Virtue differs from justice because it deals with one's moral state, while justice deals with one's relations with others. Universal justice is that state of a person who is generally lawful and fair. Particular justice deals with the "divisible" goods of honor, money, and safety, where one person's gain of such goods results in a corresponding loss by someone else.

There are two forms of particular justice: distributive and rectificatory. Distributive justice deals with the distribution of wealth among the members of a community. It employs geometric proportion: what each person receives is directly proportional to his or her merit, so a good person will receive more than a bad person. This justice is a virtuous mean between the vices of giving more than a person deserves and giving less.

Rectificatory justice remedies unequal distributions of gain and loss between two people. Rectification may be called for in cases of injustice involving voluntary transactions like trade or involuntary transactions like theft or assault. Justice is restored in a court case, where the judge ensures that the gains and losses of both parties are equaled out, thus restoring a mean.

Justice must be distributed proportionately. For instance, a shoemaker and a farmer cannot exchange one shoe for one harvest, since shoes and harvests are not of equal value. Rather, the shoemaker would have to give a number of shoes proportional in value to the crops the farmer provides. Money reflects the demand placed on various goods and allows for just exchanges.

NICOMACHEAN ETHICS ❦ 31

Political justice and domestic justice are related but distinct. Political justice is governed by the rule of law, while domestic justice relies more on respect. Political justice is based in part on natural law, which is the same for all people, and in part on particular legal conventions, which vary from place to place.

An agent is responsible only for acts of injustice performed voluntarily. We call injustice done out of ignorance "mistakes," injustice done because plans went awry "misadventures," and injustice done knowingly but without premeditation "injuries." Ignorance is an excuse only if it is reasonably unavoidable.

Aristotle reasons that no one can willingly suffer an injustice and that when goods are unjustly distributed, the distributor is more culpable than the person who receives the largest share. People mistakenly think that justice is an easy matter, as it simply requires obedience to laws. However, true justice comes only from a virtuous disposition, and those lacking in virtue are unable to perceive the just course of action in all cases.

Laws may not always be perfectly applicable. In particular circumstances in which the laws do not produce perfect justice, equity is necessary to mend the imbalance. Therefore, equity is superior to legal justice but inferior to absolute justice.

It is impossible to treat oneself unjustly. Injustice involves one person gaining at another's expense, so it requires at least two people. Even in the case of suicide, it is not the victim, but the state, that suffers an injustice.

---

## ANALYSIS

Justice, for Aristotle, consists of restoring or maintaining a proper balance. He hardly distinguishes the justice that deals with criminal cases and the justice involved in legal commerce except to call the former "involuntary" and the latter "voluntary."

It might be difficult to see what a commercial transaction might have in common with a brutal assault. For Aristotle, they both involve exchanges between two people in which one person stands to gain unfair advantage and the other stands to receive an equivalent disadvantage. Since justice deals with maintaining a proper balance, any case that might result in unfair advantage or disadvantage is a concern of justice.

Though Aristotle considers justice to be a virtue, it is not listed in his table of virtues and vices because it is a special case. Because just behavior *is* virtuous behavior, justice encompasses all the other virtues. Further, it is not the mean between two extremes—injustice itself is a single extreme.

The earlier suggestion that justice involves restoring or ensuring balance fits very nicely with Aristotle's Doctrine of the Mean. Justice is a mean state of people having their proper due, while injustice involves people having either too much or too little.

At the outset, Aristotle distinguishes between universal justice, which is a general trait of the virtuous character, and particular justice, which is the primary concern of Book V. Particular justice deals with honor, money, and safety because these are "zero sum" goods. That is, a gain for one person results in a corresponding loss for another. This is most obvious with money. If I steal fifty dollars from you, my unjust gain of fifty dollars corresponds to your unjust loss of fifty dollars. The same idea can be applied more problematically to honor and safety. Presumably, honors unjustly conferred on one person mean that another is unjustly deprived of these honors. An assault on an enemy ensures one's safety to the extent that it hurts the enemy's safety.

Because particular justice involves this zero sum exchange of goods, Aristotle associates particular injustice with greed or the desire to have more than one's due. In Chapter 2, Aristotle points out that someone who commits adultery for the sake of gain is behaving unjustly, but someone who actually loses money by committing adultery out of lust is exhibiting the vice of licentiousness, not injustice.

This notion of zero sum exchange is problematic for a number of reasons. Most obviously, especially in the case of safety, it is far from clear that one person's gain is always equal to another person's loss. If I steal an item of great personal value to you, your loss far exceeds my gain.

More significant, though, is the implication that if one person is treated unjustly, then another person must have acted unjustly toward that person. Aristotle has made it clear that injustice is a result of wanting more than one's fair share and has stated explicitly that behavior motivated by lust or anger is not unjust but rather licentious or irascible. Presumably, a person can suffer a loss, and hence suffer an injustice, as a result of someone else's lust, anger, or cowardice. The idea that justice is a zero sum game, where one person's loss is always another's gain, is thus not entirely consistent with Aristotle's discussion of virtue.

Distributive justice is a central notion in Aristotle's *Politics* but gets only a brief mention here. Aristotle's suggestion is that wealth and honor be distributed according to virtue. The most virtuous people make the most significant contributions to the life of the city, so they have the right to the greatest honors.

Distributive justice reinforces Aristotle's aristocratic bias. Women, working men, and slaves do not have the freedom to fully exercise all the virtues, so they will necessarily receive a lesser share of the city's wealth. Distributive justice is somewhat circular in this sense: those who have the greatest privilege have the greatest access to the leisure, freedom, and wealth necessary for virtue, and so are most deserving of their great privilege.

Aristotle would have seen his distributive justice not as reinforcing an unjust aristocracy but as ensuring the best form of aristocracy. That male aristocrats should rule is pretty much unquestioned by Aristotle. His concern is that the right male aristocrats should rule. His concept of distributive justice is meant to ensure that the greatest privilege go to those male aristocrats who exhibit the greatest virtue rather than to those who have the greatest wealth, the greatest military strength, or the most friends. Aristotle sees himself as trying to defend just institutions, not as trying to perpetuate injustice.

# BOOK VI

SUMMARY
We have been told that virtue comes about by choosing a mean between vicious extremes according to the right principle. This is only as helpful as telling a sick person that health comes about by choosing medicine according to what a doctor might prescribe. That is, we have no helpful understanding of virtue until we learn what this right principle is. To learn about the right principle, we must examine the intellectual virtues.

The soul is divided into a rational part and an irrational part. The rational part can be further divided into a contemplative part, which studies the invariable truths of science and mathematics, and a calculative part, which deals with the practical matters of human life. Right reasoning with respect to the contemplative intellect corresponds to truth. With the practical intellect, right reasoning corresponds to proper deliberation that leads to making the right choice.

There are five intellectual virtues by which the soul arrives at truth. First, scientific knowledge arrives at eternal truths by means of deduction or induction. Second, art or technical skill involves production according to proper reasoning. Third, prudence or practical wisdom helps us to pursue the good life generally. Fourth, intuition helps us to grasp first principles from which we derive scientific truths. Fifth, wisdom is a combination of scientific knowledge and intuition, which helps us arrive at the highest truths of all. Political science is a species of prudence, since it involves ensuring the good life for an entire city.

Resourcefulness, or good deliberation, is not the same thing as scientific knowledge, opinion, or conjecture. It is a process that helps achieve the ends envisaged by prudence. Understanding is a form of judgment regarding practical matters, which helps us determine what is equitable. Judgment, understanding, prudence, and intuition are all natural gifts that help us determine the right course of action.

The intellectual virtues help us to know what is just and admirable, and the moral virtues help us to do just and admirable deeds. We might wonder what value the intellectual virtues have, then, since knowledge is useless without action. First, the intellectual virtues lead to happiness, and so are ends in themselves. Second, the intellectual virtues help us determine the best means to the ends at which the moral virtues teach us to aim. Without prudence and cleverness, a well-disposed person can never be truly virtuous, because these intellectual virtues help us grasp the right principles of action.

## ANALYSIS

At the beginning of Book II, Aristotle distinguishes between moral virtues, which we learn through habit and practice, and intellectual virtues, which we learn through instruction. Books II to V deal with the moral virtues. Book VI turns to intellectual virtues.

Within intellectual virtue, Aristotle distinguishes the contemplative from the calculative. Contemplative reasoning deals with eternal truths. For Aristotle, these are truths unrelated to human action, as revealed in the natural sciences and mathematics. Contemplative reasoning makes use of the intellectual virtues of scientific knowledge, intuition, and wisdom. Scientific knowledge consists mostly of logical inferences derived from first principles. These first principles cannot themselves be inferred through scientific reasoning, but can be grasped only through intuition.

Wisdom is a combination of intuition and scientific knowledge, involving a deep understanding of the natural world. The Greek word for wisdom is *sophia,* and our word *philosopher* literally means "lover of wisdom." Wisdom is the highest of all intellectual virtues, because it involves a profound understanding of the eternal truths of the universe. Such understanding is brought about by philosophy. Though Aristotle thinks his work on ethics and politics is important, he rates his work on science, metaphysics, and logic as much more important.

However, the *Ethics* is concerned with the practical and noneternal matters of the human world, so contemplative reasoning receives relatively brief mention. So does art, or technical skill, which is important mostly to artists and artisans, and does not fall within the scope of the *Ethics*. Art, or technical skill, guides us in the correct manner of producing things. Prudence, or practical wisdom, guides us in the correct manner of action. This intellectual virtue, which is closely tied to the rational deliberation and choice necessary to the moral virtues, is the central focus of Aristotle's discussion of the intellectual virtues in the *Ethics*.

The Greek word translated as "prudence" or "practical wisdom" is *phronesis,* which conveys a general sense of knowing the proper behavior in all situations. *Phronesis* is an intellectual virtue rather than a moral virtue because we learn it through instruction and not practice, but it is very closely connected to the moral virtues. Without *phronesis,* it would be impossible to practice the moral virtues properly. A person who has all the right moral virtues knows what ends to pursue, but without *phronesis,* that person will not know how to set about pursuing the right ends. Contrary to modern assumptions, Aristotle is telling us that having one's heart in the right place is not good enough: being a good person requires a kind of practical intelligence as well as a good disposition.

On the other hand, a person who has *phronesis* but does not have the right moral virtues will be very effective in devising means to personal ends, but those ends might not be noble. The villain in a James Bond film might be seen as a portrait of a person with *phronesis* but no moral virtue.

The logical syllogism, which was invented and perfected by Aristotle, consists of three terms: a major premise, which states some general truth; a minor premise, which states some particular truth; and a conclusion. For instance, the major premise "all humans are mammals" and the minor premise "Aristotle is a human" lead to the conclusion "Aristotle is a mammal." Aristotle takes the syllogism to be the basic unit of reasoning and applies it not only to reasoning in the sciences but also to practical reasoning.

*Phronesis,* then, consists of practical syllogisms with three terms. The major premise states some general practical truth—for example, "Always hold the door open for elderly people." The minor premise states a particular fact related to the major premise—for example, "An elderly person is coming toward this door." The conclusion is the action that the major and minor premises entail—in other words, holding the door open for the elderly person.

The practical syllogism cannot be completed without both moral virtue and *phronesis*. Moral virtue supplies us with the appropriate major premises, and *phronesis* helps us to move from the major premise to an appropriate course of action. Without *phronesis*, the virtuous person would not necessarily know how to act, and without moral virtue, the clever person would not always pursue the appropriate ends.

# BOOK VII

## SUMMARY

There are three bad states of character: vice, incontinence, and brutishness. Opposite to these three are virtue, continence, and superhuman virtue. We now examine incontinence and softness, or effeminacy, and their opposites, continence and endurance.

A great deal of inconsistency exists among popular views about incontinence. How does incontinence arise: is it through ignorance or in full knowledge? With respect to what are people incontinent? How does incontinence differ from vices like licentiousness?

Aristotle proposes four solutions. First, it is possible that a person knows what is wrong but does not reflect upon this knowledge, and so does wrong without thinking about it. Second, the incontinent person may make a false inference when using the practical syllogism due to ignorance of the facts. Third, the incontinent person may be emotionally excited or mentally disturbed and therefore unable to think clearly. Fourth, desire may cause a person to act hastily without self-restraint or more careful reasoning.

A person who shows excessive desire for the pleasures of victory, honor, or wealth is called incontinent with qualification: "incontinent with respect to victory," for example. By contrast, a person who shows excessive desire for bodily pleasure, such as sex or food, is simply called incontinent without qualification. Incontinence with qualification is not real incontinence, but is only called incontinence by analogy to incontinence without qualification. Licentiousness and incontinence are closely connected, though the licentious person acts out of choice while the incontinent person lacks such self-control.

It is more forgivable to be incontinent as a result of temper than desire. A person with a short temper is reasonable up to a point, but the person who gives in to desire is entirely unreasonable. Furthermore, being incontinent is better than being licentious, since it is better to do bad things from lack of self-control than from conscious choice. Continence is preferable to endurance, since continence involves conquering the pull of desires rather than just enduring them. The opposite of endurance is softness or effeminacy, where a person is unable to bear the sorts of pains most people can.

The licentious person is more easily reformed than the incontinent person, because he or she acts from choice and can be reasoned with. The licentious person is wicked, while the incontinent person does wicked things without being willfully wicked.

Many philosophers are critical of pleasure. Some say that pleasure is always bad, arguing that temperate and prudent people avoid pleasure, that pleasure clouds sensible thought and distracts us from our proper ends. Others say that some pleasures are disgraceful or harmful. Yet others say that pleasure cannot be the supreme good, since it is not an end in itself, but a process.

Aristotle responds that pleasure is an activity, hence an end, not a process. Pleasure is harmful only in a limited sense, while the highest pleasures, such as contemplation, are not harmful in any sense. In fact, achieving the supreme end of a good life is a pleasurable activity, and we seek the good life precisely because it is pleasurable. This kind of pleasure is the highest good of all. Pleasures of the body are bad only if taken to excess. Nonetheless, pleasures of the mind are preferrable.

---

## ANALYSIS

Socrates claimed that no one knowingly does wrong. In his view, any wrongdoing results from ignorance of one kind or another. The goal of moral education, then, is to ensure that everyone knows what is good and why it is good so that no one will be susceptible to the sorts of ignorance that lead to wrongdoing.

Aristotle accepts Socrates' thesis but realizes that it calls for some detailed elaboration. Not all bad behavior is the same, so there must be various kinds of ignorance, some more culpable than others.

Aristotle identifies three major sources of wrongdoing: vice, incontinence, and brutishness. Vice is the opposite of virtue. Like virtue, it is developed from a young age through habit and practice. Also like virtue, vice is a disposition to behave in a certain way. A person with the virtue of temperance is disposed to behave temperately and will think of temperance as the correct form of behavior. By contrast, a person with the vice of licentiousness is deposed to behave licentiously, and will think of this licentiousness as the correct form of behavior. Vice is therefore the worst of the three sources of wrongdoing, since a person who acts out of vice acts voluntarily and deliberately: having thought about a particular act, this person has decided that it is the right thing to do.

The incontinent person differs from the vicious person, then, in that the incontinent person knows what is good but does wrong anyway. An incontinent person might have the virtue of temperance and know that licentious behavior is blameworthy, but still lack the self-control to resist licentious behavior. Incontinence is not as bad as vice, since it is more a form of weakness than actual moral badness.

Brutishness is an extreme form of irrational wrongdoing. A brute lacks the capacity for rational thought altogether and so has no sense of what is right or wrong. With characteristically Greek xenophobia, Aristotle suggests that brutishness is most common among non-Greeks but remarks that brutish behavior can also be found in the mentally ill and other unbalanced characters.

"Incontinence" is a vague definition of the Greek word *akrasia,* which is more accurately but more cumbersomely translated as "lacking self-control." *Akrasia* is particularly puzzling for anyone who accepts Socrates' claim, since the person who does wrong out of *akrasia* does so with full knowledge of the wrongdoing. If Socrates is right and no one knowingly does wrong, how are we to account for *akrasia*?

*Akrasia* involves giving in to guilty pleasures, so it should come as no surprise that we find an analysis of pleasure in the book that deals with *akrasia*. Aristotle is much more approving of pleasure than Plato and Plato's followers, and he defends pleasure on a number of counts. According to Plato, pleasure comes from a process of restoration. For instance, we get pleasure from eating because we are restoring our bodies from a state of hunger to a state of satiation. For Plato, then, pleasure cannot possibly be the supreme good, since it is only good at all when we are in a less than ideal state. At best, it is a process that helps us reach a better state, but then we should value that better state and not the process that leads us there.

Aristotle disagrees fundamentally with Plato's analysis of pleasure, arguing that it is an activity, or *energeia,* and not a process. For instance, we get pleasure from listening to good music not because listening brings us to some desirable end state, but because listening is an activity worthwhile in itself. Recall that in Book I, Aristotle also describes happiness as an activity. For Aristotle, the good life is not an end state that we are constantly striving for, but rather a way of living that consists of habitually virtuous activities. Pleasure is not incidental to the good life; it is the feeling of satisfaction we have when living well.

Only truly virtuous people take pleasure in the right things, however. Neither the incontinent nor the continent person has this kind of virtue. Both have formed bad habits and are tempted to take pleasure in the wrong sorts of activities. The continent person differs from the incontinent in that he or she is able to control these temptations.

*Akrasia,* then, is a result of poorly formed habits, like vice. Unlike vice, though, *akrasia* involves an intellectual understanding of what is right. In Aristotle's view, it is possible to do wrong while knowing what is right, because the intellect does not always have full control over the mind's lower functions. In this respect, Aristotle represents a modification of the Socratic view, maintaining still that wrongdoing consists of a kind of ignorance, but suggesting also that perfect rationality is not a foolproof shield against wrongdoing.

## BOOK VIII

*Friendliness is considered to be justice in the fullest sense.*          (*See* QUOTATIONS, *p. 54*)

### SUMMARY

Friendship is clearly necessary and splendid, but people disagree on its precise nature. Friendship consists of a mutual feeling of goodwill between two people.

There are three kinds of friendship. The first is friendship based on utility, where both people derive some benefit from each other. The second is friendship based on pleasure, where both people are drawn to the other's wit, good looks, or other pleasant qualities. The third is friendship based on goodness, where both people admire the other's goodness and help one another strive for goodness.

The first two kinds of friendship are only accidental, because in these cases friends are motivated by their own utility and pleasure, not by anything essential to the nature of the friend. Both of these kinds of friendship are short-lived because one's needs and pleasures are apt to change over time.

Goodness is an enduring quality, so friendships based on goodness tend to be long lasting. This friendship encompasses the other two, as good friends are useful to one another and please one another. Such friendship is rare and takes time to develop, but it is the best. Bad people can be friends for reasons of pleasure or utility, but only good people can be friends for each other's sake.

On the whole, friendships consist of equal exchanges, whether of utility, pleasantness, or goodness. However, there are some relationships that by their nature exist between two people of unequal standing: father-son, husband-wife, ruler-subject. In these relationships, a different kind of love is called for from each party, and the amount of love should be proportional to the merit of each person. For instance, a subject should show more love for a ruler than the the reverse. When there is too great a gap between people, friendship is impossible, and often two friends will grow apart if one becomes far more virtuous than the other.

Most people prefer being loved to loving, since they desire flattery and honor. The true mark of friendship, though, is that it consists more of loving than of being loved. Friendships endure when each friend loves the other according to the other's merit.

Justice and friendship are closely connected, as both tie communities together. Since justice, friendship, and community are closely related, it is far worse to abuse a close friend or family member than it is to abuse a stranger.

There are three kinds of political constitution: monarchy, aristocracy, and timocracy. Tyranny is the corruption of monarchy, where the tyrant looks out for his own interest rather than that of his subjects. Oligarchy is a perversion of aristocracy, and democracy is a perversion of timocracy, but neither is as bad as tyranny. Monarchy is analogous to the father-son relationship, aristocracy to the husband-wife relationship, and timocracy to the relationship between brothers. Corrupt political institutions are like those relationships where no friendship exists, as in the master-slave relationship.

Problems between friends occur most frequently within friendships based on utility. On the whole, the person who receives a service, and not the giver, should determine the value of that service. In unequal friendship, it is important that each person receive an appropriate benefit. A poor person cannot give money to a rich benefactor, but can give whatever honor is within the poor person's means.

## ANALYSIS

In discussing friendship, Aristotle seems intent on discussing every kind of interpersonal relationship and deals at some length with family relationships and political institutions. Nonetheless, his model of ideal friendship is that which exists between two aristocratic men of great virtue. These men are not bonded together through need, utility, or familial duty, but rather through mutual respect and virtue.

Aristotle explains that friendship is the act of loving rather than the act of being loved. It is important that friendship be active, since Aristotle treats friendship as an *energeia*, akin to pleasure and happiness. Friendship is one of the essential components of the good life, and the value of friendship is in having and enjoying it.

While we in the modern world certainly place a high premium on friendship, it carries far more importance for Aristotle. Flipping through modern works on ethics, it would be difficult to find an extended discussion of friendship at all, let alone a discussion that occupies one-fifth of an exhaustive treatment of the subject, as Aristotle's does. Friendship no longer carries significant philosophical importance to us because we live in a world where individualism predominates. While most of us are not singlemindedly selfish, we generally assume that we each choose our own path in life, which is defined by a personal set of goals and values. Friends are a help and a comfort along the way, but we cannot expect them to share all our goals and values.

Aristotle's worldview is significantly different because he thinks of human life as having a *telos*, or end goal, toward which it is heading. In Aristotle's world, city-states are tightly knit communities where no strong distinction exists between public and private life. All citizens share the same goals and values, so the pursuit of happiness is a cooperative enterprise.

The close connection between friendship, the community, and the individual explains why we find a discussion of political constitutions in the middle of Book VIII. According to Aristotle, citizens should not cooperate simply because the laws compel them to. Rather, they should cooperate out of a friendly feeling that comes from sharing their lives and goals with one another. His analogies between political relationships and family relationships are not simply metaphorical: both should be determined primarily by love and duty. Laws exist only as safeguards for when the appropriate friendly feelings break down.

Aristotle discusses political constitutions in much greater detail in the *Politics,* which does not agree entirely with his assessment in the *Ethics.* In that work, he describes oligarchy as the corrupt form of aristocracy, and he is not so firm in his claim that monarchy is superior to aristocracy and timocracy.

Timocracy, which in the *Politics* is called a polity or constitutional government, derives its name from the Greek word *teme,* meaning property qualification. The idea is that all citizens with a minimal property qualification have equal rights. This is roughly the form of government that existed in Athens.

Monarchy, aristocracy, and timocracy are all considered to be good forms of government because they all extend privileges according to merit. In a monarchy, the king is of more noble stature than any of his subjects, and so he has every right to govern absolutely so long as he cares for them. An aristocracy consists of a small ruling elite who again are the most noble, and a timocracy also proffers benefits according to each person's due. This conferring of benefits according to merit is the principle of distributive justice, which Aristotle discusses in Book V.

When merit ceases to determine privilege in a state, that state slides from one of these forms of government to a corrupt form. For instance, a tyrant is a king who no longer cares for his subjects and so is no longer virtuous and worthy of his place.

It may seem strange that Aristotle lists democracy among the corrupt forms of government, as we generally think of democracy as one of the greatest inventions of the Greeks. Aristotle uses "democracy" to mean a kind of mob rule, where those who are afforded the most privilege are not necessarily those who most deserve this privilege.

# BOOK IX

## SUMMARY

In friendships or exchanges where each person receives a different benefit, it is important that both parties feel they are being justly treated. The best method is to fix a price in advance, though some forms of benevolence cannot properly be repaid. In cases of dispute, the recipient of a service should determine its value. While it is important to show preference to one's friends, one should not do so in place of meeting obligations to others.

Friendships based on utility or pleasure dissolve when the friends no longer find utility or pleasure in one another. These breakups are made more complicated when people are misled into thinking they are loved for their character and not for certain incidental attributes. It may also be necessary to break off a friendship with some-one who initially misrepresented the kind of person he or she really is. Friends who grow apart cannot remain friends, though they should hold on to some consideration for the former friendship.

The feelings we have for our friends are the same as we have for ourselves. For instance, a good friend wishes good things for his or her friend, enjoys that friend's company, and shares personal joys and sorrows. This can also be said of our relationship with our-selves, even in the case of bad people, who treat both themselves and their friends poorly.

We feel goodwill toward a person in whom we perceive some merit or goodness, but this feeling is different from friendship or even affection, because it is superficial and not necessarily requited. Concord is a form of friendly feeling that exists between friends or within a state when people have the same ends in view.

Benefactors seem to love those whom they have benefited more than the beneficiaries love in return. This love is like the love of an artist for his or her work, because the benefactor is to some extent responsible for "making" the beneficiary. It is also more pleasurable to do good actively than to receive good passively.

Those who denigrate self-love are thinking of people who seek the greatest honors and pleasures only for themselves. A good per-son who is self-loving will seek only what is best for himself or her-self, which will be consistent with what is best for all. A good person will do seemingly unselfish acts, such as taking risks for friends or giving away money, but will do these things because they are noble and are motivated by self-love.

If a good person is self-sufficient, it follows that he or she has no need of friends. However, friendship is one of the greatest goods in life, so a good person cannot achieve perfect happiness without friends.

Obviously, it is better to have many friends, but there is a limit to how many intimate friendships one can sustain, and it is preferable to have a few close friendships than many superficial friendships. While we need friends more in adversity, friendship is more pleasant in prosperity. In adversity, we do not want others to share our misfortunes, and in prosperity we can help others.

## ANALYSIS

Aristotle's discussion of friendship, coupled with his earlier discussion of happiness and virtue, seems to imply two difficult paradoxes. First, if we admire friends for those qualities we admire in ourselves, it would seem that self-love is more important than the love of others. Second, if self-love is the most important thing, and if the truly happy person is not in need of outside help, it would seem that the truly happy person does not need friends at all.

Aristotle's answer to the first paradox is that self-love is indeed very valuable: it seems like a negative quality only because we are thinking of the wrong kind of person. In Book VIII, Aristotle distinguishes three different kinds of friendship: friendship based on utility, friendship based on pleasure, and friendship based on goodness of character. Similarly, self-love can take on any of these characteristics. We think of self-love as a bad thing because we normally think of it in terms of utility or pleasure. The person who selfishly seeks the benefits of utility will callously seek out wealth and honor, not caring who is crushed along the way. The person who selfishly seeks the benefits of pleasure will callously seek out sex, good food, and other pleasures, not caring who gets hurt along the way.

These are both inferior forms of self-love, according to Aristotle. People who seek only utility or pleasure for themselves are not treating themselves well, just as people who use friends for utility or pleasure are not treating those friends well. It is best to love a friend for that friend's good character, and that is also the best reason to love oneself. The person who seeks true personal goodness will aim at a virtuous life that consists not only of health and prosperity, but also of magnanimity and amiability.

Aristotle's ideal of the virtuous self-lover is not far removed from our own ideals of selfless virtue, though there are important differences. Both the self-lover and the selfless person will look out for the benefit of others. However, Aristotle's self-lover will look out for others, recognizing this concern as a noble personal trait, while selfless people do not think of themselves at all. Aristotle would not hold Mother Theresa in high esteem. The kindness of a self-lover is more a *noblesse oblige,* where the kindness of the noble man is given with the understanding that he is noble and superior to the people he is helping.

Aristotle's discussion of self-love marks him as one of the early proponents of ethical egoism, a controversial issue in the modern world. Ethical egoism is the idea that self-love is the most important virtue and that if we all sought what was best for ourselves, the world would naturally work its way into a desirable shape without the need for selflessness. This idea is unpopular in the modern world because its most ardent proponents tend to be selfish conservatives who have no interest in the needs of others. Unlike us, however, Aristotle lived in a world where there was common agreement on what was good for all and where the community mattered more than the individual. In such a world, successful people measured their success in part by the success of their fellow citizens. Selfishness seems like a vice only in a world driven by individualism, where there is no evident benefit for oneself in helping others.

When we understand the communal nature of ancient Greek society, we are much closer to understanding the value of friendship as well. In the *Politics*, Aristotle argues that a man cannot live a complete life outside a city-state, because the exercise of civic virtue is a part of living a complete life. Since living among others is an essential component to life, it follows that one cannot live a complete life without the benefit of friendship.

While it is helpful to understand Aristotle's views on friendship and self-love within their proper contexts, there is still something troubling about ethical egoism. Presumably, the good person does good for others not primarily because of concern for others, but because of concern for self. This idea hearkens back to the virtue of magnanimity: the virtuous person knows himself to be virtuous and expects others to respect him for being virtuous. Such a person is perhaps not morally objectionable, but there is a degree of shallowness to being good only for the sake of being good and not for the sake of what comes from being good.

# BOOK X

> *The intellect is the highest thing in us, and the objects*
> *that it apprehends are the highest things that can be*
> *known . . . we are more capable of continuous*
> *contemplation than we are of any practical activity.*
> (See QUOTATIONS, p. 55)

## SUMMARY

Eudoxus, a member of Plato's Academy, argues that pleasure is the supreme good because we desire it as an end in itself and it makes other good things more desirable. However, this only shows that pleasure is *a* good. Further, Plato argues that other things, like intelligence, make pleasure more desirable, so it cannot be the supreme good. There are also flaws in the arguments that all, or even some, pleasures are bad. These arguments rely on the mistaken notion that pleasure is an incomplete process of replenishment.

We cannot say that pleasure is desirable without qualification: for instance, we would not choose to live with the mentality of a child even if that life were pleasant. There are also other goods, like intelligence or good eyesight, which are desirable without necessarily being pleasant. It seems clear that not all pleasures are desirable and that pleasure is not the supreme Good.

Pleasure is not a process, since it is not a movement from incompleteness to completeness and does not necessarily take place over an extended period of time. Rather, pleasure accompanies the activity of any of our faculties, like the senses or the mind, when they are working at their best. Pleasure perfects our activities, and since life itself is an activity, pleasure is essential to life. Only those pleasures enjoyed by a good person and for the right reasons are good.

Happiness, as an activity that serves as an end in itself, is our highest goal in life. We should not confuse happiness with pleasant amusement, though.

The highest form of happiness is contemplation. Contemplation is an activity of our highest rational faculties, and it is an end in itself, unlike many of our practical activities. Only a god could spend an entire lifetime occupied with nothing but contemplation, but we should try to approximate this godlike activity as best we can. All the moral virtues deal with the human aspects of life, which are necessary but secondary to the divine activity of contemplation.

If learning about happiness were sufficient to leading a good life, discourses in philosophy would be far more valuable than they are. Words alone cannot convince people to be good: this requires practice and habituation, and can take seed only in a person of good character.

People are unlikely to be naturally virtuous, so the state is responsible for establishing laws to ensure that the young are educated in the right way and that adults do not become bad. In the absence of good laws, people must take responsibility for their children and friends. Parental supervision is in many ways preferable to laws, since it allows for more particularized attention.

Neither politicians nor sophists are particularly suited to teaching politics. In order to judge how best to establish laws that will benefit citizens, we must turn to an examination of politics.

---

## ANALYSIS

It might seem strange that we have a discussion of pleasure at the beginning of Book X, when this topic was already addressed in Book VII. There are two answers to this peculiarity. The first is that Book VII and Book X were most likely written at different times and for different purposes, and were only later interpolated into the same book. Books V, VI, and VII of the *Nicomachean Ethics* also feature in the *Eudemian Ethics*, which is Aristotle's other, less known work on ethics. These two works were probably composed at different points in Aristotle's career, and it is possible that the compiler of the *Nicomachean Ethics* took these three books from the *Eudemian Ethics* and inserted them into a significantly different work.

The different times of composition also explains why Aristotle's views on pleasure differ somewhat between Books VII and X. Most notably, Aristotle implies that pleasure is supremely good in Book VII, but in Book X he is more reserved on this point, noting that certain good things, like excellent eyesight or intelligence, are not necessarily pleasant. Perhaps good eyesight and intelligence bring us pleasure from time to time, but there is nothing about seeing well that is in itself always pleasant. Though there is some debate on this topic, most scholars agree that Book X represents Aristotle's more mature views on pleasure.

The second explanation of the disparity between Books VII and X is that they deal with different subject matter. The discussion of pleasure in Book VII follows a discussion of incontinence and is meant to illuminate what pleasure is that it should lead people to act against their better judgment. The discussion of pleasure in Book X leads to a discussion of happiness and the good life, and is meant to show in what way pleasure is connected to the good life.

Book X also gives us Aristotle's ultimate judgment of what constitutes the good life. While the moral virtues are fine and important, rational contemplation is the highest activity. This may not be immediately evident, so we should first examine how Aristotle arrives at this conclusion and then question whether it is correct.

Aristotle holds teleological view of biology. That is, he believes that all living things exist to fulfill some *telos,* or purpose. This *telos* is determined primarily by what makes that living thing distinctive. For instance, the *telos* of a plant is primarily nutritive: its goal in life is to grow. Aristotle distinguishes humans from other animals by saying that we are capable of rational thought. Because we are the distinctively *rational* animals, our *telos* must be based in our rationality.

This theme underlies a great deal of the *Ethics.* In discussing voluntary action, Aristotle emphasizes choice based on rational deliberation. Our actions can be morally praiseworthy or blameworthy because we are able to think about them and decide rationally on the best course of action.

Most of the *Ethics* is devoted to discussing the various moral virtues. In the end, however, Aristotle explains that these moral virtues are not ends in themselves so much as necessary preconditions for living a good life. This good life is based on our rational faculties, which explains his discussion of the intellectual virtues in Book VI.

Of the intellectual virtues, two of them—prudence and art—are practical virtues. These help us fulfill our practical needs and so cannot be ends in themselves. Of the intellectual virtues, wisdom is the highest, since it combines the other two virtues of scientific knowledge and intuition. Scientific knowledge and intuition help us to figure out what the world is like. Wisdom consists of the ability to contemplate the totality of experience from a place of knowledge. As such, wisdom represents the most achieved state of the rational intellect.

Because wisdom is the highest intellectual virtue, and because the rational uses of the intellect are the highest human goal, the philosophical contemplation made possible by wisdom is the supreme human achievement. While this contemplation could be called "philosophy," we should be careful to note that for the Greeks, philosophy consists of a contemplation of knowledge generally, and not the more specialized study that modern philosophy consists of.

Is Aristotle right in saying that philosophical contemplation is the highest good? He certainly provides many compelling and noble reasons to think so, but he never provides a watertight argument for thinking so. We might feel inclined to respond that some of the lower pleasures are more worthwhile than solemn contemplation. To this, Aristotle might respond that we are giving into our less than human animalistic natures. But aside from feeling Aristotle's stern disapprobation, there does not seem to be any compelling reason to think that a little animalistic fun is not in itself sometimes quite worthwhile.

# Important Quotations Explained

1. Our account of this science will be adequate if it achieves such clarity as the subject-matter allows; for the same degree of precision is not to be expected in all discussions, any more than in all products of handicraft.

This statement, which appears in Book I, Chapter 3, is the first of a number of caveats with which Aristotle warns us not to expect any precise rules or codes of conduct. This is not laziness on Aristotle's part, but, as he explains, the nature of the beast. Ethics deals with the vagaries of human life and must remain flexible enough to account for the great deal of variety and possibility.

Furthermore, Aristotle tells us that virtue cannot be taught in a classroom but can be learned only through constant practice until it becomes habitual. If virtue consisted of hard and fast rules, it would indeed be possible to lay them out explicitly in a classroom. Unfortunately for those hoping for the easy road to success, no such rules exist. Knowing what to do is a matter of applying *phronesis*, or prudence, on a case-by-case basis.

QUOTATIONS

2.   [T]he good for man is an activity of the soul in accordance
     with virtue, or if there are more kinds of virtue than one, in
     accordance with the best and most perfect kind.

This quotation from Book I, Chapter 7, connects Aristotle's conception of happiness and the good life with his conception of virtue. We
should observe first that "the good for man is an activity." The word
*activity* translates from the Greek *energeia*, which signifies not only
physical activity but also mental activity as seemingly inactive as
contemplation or daydreaming. The point is that the good life is not
an end state that we achieve but rather a way of life that we live. We
might consider the *cliché* "life is a journey, not a destination" to
convey some sense of the distinction Aristotle has in mind.

The bulk of the *Ethics* is devoted to discussing the various moral
and intellectual virtues. These virtues are dispositions to behave in
the correct way. They are not themselves activities, but they ensure
that our activities will be of the right kind. To live "in accordance
with virtue," then, is to live in such a way that our activities flow
naturally from a virtuous disposition.

In Books VI and X, Aristotle suggests that the intellectual virtue
of wisdom is the "best and most perfect kind" of virtue, and he ultimately concludes that the good for man is rational contemplation in
accordance with the intellectual virtue of wisdom.

3.   So virtue is a purposive disposition, lying in a mean that is
     relative to us and determined by a rational principle, by that
     which a prudent man would use to determine it.

This quotation from Book II, Chapter 6, gives us a clear expression
of Aristotle's Doctrine of the Mean: virtue is a mean disposition
between the vicious extremes of excess and deficiency. In calling virtue a "purposive" disposition, Aristotle means that virtue is not just
a disposition we sit on and do nothing about, but is rather the impe-
tus that leads us to virtuous activity.
    Aristotle gives no rules as to what counts as a mean. His reason is
that the mean depends greatly on the person and the situation.
Rather than lay down any rules, he recommends *phronesis,* or prudence, which helps us reason our way through practical matters and
determine the best course to take.

4.    Between friends there is no need for justice, but people who
      are just still need the quality of friendship; and indeed
      friendliness is considered to be justice in the fullest sense. It
      is not only a necessary thing but a splendid one.

Aristotle makes this assertion in Book VIII, Chapter 1. Neither
friendship nor justice is listed in Aristotle's table of virtues and vices,
because both are more general than the particular virtues and vices
listed there. In Book V, Aristotle explains that justice comprehends
all the virtues, since acting justly consists essentially of acting in
accordance with all the virtues.

Aristotle bases his conception of justice on a conception of fair
exchange, and does the same for friendship. Friendships are bal-
anced by the fact that each friend gives as much as receives. Hence,
justice and friendship are closely connected.

Citizens in the Greek city-states were expected to take a very
active role in the government of their city-state, so justice and civic
duty would have been a concern for all. A complete life could not
have been lived in solitude, so justice and friendliness between fellow citizens was essential.

5.     [C]ontemplation is both the highest form of activity (since the intellect is the highest thing in us, and the objects that it apprehends are the highest things that can be known), and also it is the most continuous, because we are more capable of continuous contemplation than we are of any practical activity.

Near the end of the *Ethics,* in Book X, Chapter 7, Aristotle concludes that contemplation is the highest human good. Aristotle distinguishes rationality, and the intellect in particular, as the highest human functions, since these are the functions that distinguish us from other animals. It is also through the intellect that we can think about philosophy, God, and nature, which Aristotle considers to be far more noble objects of thought than the daily matters of human society. Consequently, he reasons that a life of continuous contemplation is the best possible human life. Of course, life cannot consist solely of contemplation, since practical matters always need dealing with, but in Aristotle's view, the more contemplation the better. Practical wisdom and the moral virtues are noble and essential to securing the good life, but the good life itself consists foremost of contemplation.

# KEY FACTS

**FULL TITLE**
*Nicomachean Ethics*

**AUTHOR**
Aristotle

**TYPE OF WORK**
Philosophical treatise

**LANGUAGE**
Ancient (Classical or Attic) Greek

**TIME AND PLACE WRITTEN**
Between 334 and 323 B.C. in Athens; composed as lecture notes
for Aristotle's courses at the Lyceum

**DATE OF FIRST PUBLICATION**
Compiled by editors an indeterminate, short time after
Aristotle's death

**NARRATOR**
The *Ethics* are notes from Aristotle's lectures, so the speaker is
undoubtedly Aristotle himself

**MAJOR TOPICS**
Virtue and happiness; moral education; the doctrine of the mean;
the unity of the virtues; the importance of friendship; the life of
contemplation

# STUDY QUESTIONS & ESSAY TOPICS

## STUDY QUESTIONS

1. *In what ways does the Greek concept of* EUDAIMONIA
   *differ from our own concept of happiness?*

Primarily, the Greek concept of *eudaimonia* is a much more public matter than our concept of happiness. We tend to think of happiness as an emotional state, whereas the Greeks treat *eudaimonia* as a measure of objective success. It would be unthinkable for a Greek that a beggar could have *eudaimonia,* while a successful business-man and eminent public figure could suffer from depression and still have *eudaimonia.*

2. *What is Aristotle's Doctrine of the Mean? In what ways
   is it different from the Christian conception of virtue?*

The Doctrine of the Mean maintains that virtue is a mean state between the vicious extremes of excess and deficiency. While this does not provide us with a strict formulation, it does make clear that finding the virtuous path is a matter of steering a middle course between the vices of too much and too little. Because both excess and deficiency are vices, Aristotle's virtues and vices are listed in threes: a vice of excess and a vice of deficiency to accompany each virtue.

By contrast, Christian conceptions of virtue are generally based on polar oppositions and are classed in pairs. For instance, the virtue of humility is contrasted with the vice of pride. The marked difference between Aristotle's and the Christian beliefs, then, is that for Aristotle, vice and virtue are intimately connected. The virtuous disposition that might lead a person to be courageous can be taken just a little too far and become the vice of rashness. A Christian virtue cannot be "taken too far" and become a vice, since vice is an opposite to virtue in the Christian view.

3. *How does Aristotle define moral responsibility? Why*
   *does he not define free will? How might he define free*
   *will?*

Aristotle gives us a negative definition of moral responsibility. He
tells us that we are responsible for those actions we do voluntarily,
and then tells us that involuntary actions are those done out of ignorance or compulsion. There are some gray areas as to what counts as
excusable ignorance and what counts as forgivable compulsion, but
we are told effectively that we are responsible for all our actions that
are not performed in ignorance or under compulsion.

Aristotle's interest is solely in when and how to assign praise and
blame. He is not concerned with the metaphysical or psychological
questions of what motivates blameworthy action or to what extent it is
preventable. As such, he takes no interest in the question of free will.

It would be anachronistic to assign a theory of free will to Aristotle, since the will generally finds no significant application in his philosophy. However, it might make sense to borrow from his
distinction between voluntary and involuntary action, and suggest
that free will consists of the freedom to act voluntarily.

# Suggested Essay Topics

1. *How does Aristotle's list of virtues and vices differ from our modern conceptions of vice and virtue? How might we determine which is better: Aristotle's system or our own?*

2. *What is distributive justice? What are the pros and cons of this form of justice?*

3. *What is the role of practical wisdom, or PHRONESIS? How does it mediate between the moral virtues and the intellectual virtues?*

4. *What is incontinence, or AKRASIA? How can a person know what is right and still do what is wrong?*

5. *Why is friendship so important to Aristotle?*

6. *What is ethical egoism? Do you agree with Aristotle's endorsement of it? Why or why not?*

7. *What, according to Aristotle, is the supreme human activity? What arguments does he give for this position?*

# Review & Resources

1. Which of the following words is *not* a plausible translation of *eudaimonia*?

   A. Happiness
   B. Virtue
   C. Success
   D. Fulfillment

2. Which of the following is always an end in itself?

   A. Happiness
   B. Virtue
   C. Intelligence
   D. Honor

3. Which of the following, according to Aristotle, is the highest pursuit in life?

   A. The pursuit of pleasure
   B. The pursuit of honors
   C. The pursuit of Plato's Form of Good
   D. The pursuit of rational contemplation

4. Which of the following is *not* listed as a virtue in Aristotle's Table of Virtues and Vices?

   A. Courage
   B. Humility
   C. Patience
   D. Wittiness

5. Which of the following statements about Aristotle's Doctrine of the Mean is correct?

    A. The mean is the exact middle point between two opposing vices.
    B. Virtues and vices exist in sets of opposing pairs.
    C. The mean between two opposing vices may be much closer to one vice than the other.
    D. The virtuous mean is the same for all people.

6. How do we learn virtue?

    A. By habit
    B. By dialectical argument
    C. By rational instruction
    D. By learning from our mistakes

7. If someone does wrong out of ignorance and never comes to recognize this ignorance, how do we describe that person's action?

    A. Voluntary
    B. Involuntary
    C. Nonvoluntary
    D. None of the above

8. Which of the senses is most susceptible to licentiousness?

    A. Taste
    B. Touch
    C. Sight
    D. Smell

9. Which of the following is *not*, strictly speaking, a virtue?

    A. Wittiness
    B. Modesty
    C. Magnificence
    D. Courage

REVIEW & RESOURCES

10. Which of the following does Aristotle consider to be the worst?

    A.  Being great and expecting great honors
    B.  Being mediocre and expecting great honors
    C.  Being great and expecting moderate honors
    D.  B and C are equally bad.

11. Which of the following is *not* one of the social virtues?

    A.  Amiability
    B.  Sincerity
    C.  Wittiness
    D.  Self-deprecation

12. Which of the following is *not* a concern of particular justice?

    A.  Honor
    B.  Safety
    C.  Money
    D.  Happiness

13. How is justice different from virtue?

    A.  Virtue is just one form of justice.
    B.  Justice deals with our relations to others, while virtue is a state of being.
    C.  Justice can be a vice in the wrong hands.
    D.  Justice is a human invention while virtue exists objectively.

14. Which of the following is *not* an intellectual virtue?

    A.  Intuition
    B.  Wisdom
    C.  Wittiness
    D.  Prudence

15. Which intellectual virtue is the most important?

    A.  Prudence
    B.  Wisdom
    C.  Intuition
    D.  Scientific knowledge

16. Which of the following is most blameworthy?

    A.  Softness
    B.  Vice
    C.  Brutishness
    D.  Incontinence

17. Which of the following pleasures can be a source of incontinence without qualification?

    A.  Sex
    B.  Honor
    C.  Wealth
    D.  Victory

18. Which of the following most accurately reflects Aristotle's view of pleasure?

    A.  It is always bad.
    B.  It is a process of restoration.
    C.  It distracts us and keeps us from thinking straight.
    D.  The pleasure of a virtuous person is the supreme good.

19. What is the best form of friendship based upon?

    A.  Utility
    B.  Pleasure
    C.  Goodness
    D.  Law

20. Which is the best kind of political constitution, according to the *Ethics*?

    A.  Monarchy
    B.  Aristocracy
    C.  Timocracy
    D.  Democracy

21. Which of the following relationships is analogous to the king-subject relationship?

    A. Husband-wife
    B. Father-son
    C. Master-slave
    D. Brother-sister

22. How should one treat an old friend whom one has long since exceeded in friendship?

    A. Remain friends as always.
    B. Remain friends, but not as closely as before.
    C. Break off the friendship, but maintain feelings of goodwill for the old friend.
    D. Break off all relations with the old friend.

23. What does Aristotle claim to be the highest human activity?

    A. Political science
    B. Friendship
    C. Contemplation
    D. Prudence

24. Who are the best teachers of political science?

    A. Sophists
    B. Politicians
    C. Friends
    D. None of the above

25. Which of the following concepts does Aristotle *not* advocate?

    A. Distributive justice
    B. Ethical egoism
    C. Democracy
    D. Happiness as the highest good

**ANSWER KEY:**

1: B; 2: A; 3: D; 4: B; 5: C; 6: A; 7: C; 8: B; 9: B; 10: C; 11: D; 12: D; 13: B; 14: C; 15: B; 16: B; 17: A; 18: D; 19: C; 20: A; 21: B; 22: C; 23: C; 24: D; 25: C

# SUGGESTIONS FOR FURTHER READING

AUSTIN, J. L. "*Agathon* and *Eudaimonia* in the *Ethics* of Aristotle" in *Philosophical Papers*. Oxford, Oxford University Press, 1970.

BARNES, JONATHAN. *Aristotle*. Oxford, Oxford University Press, 2000.

DUNNE, JOSEPH. *Back to the Rough Ground: "Phronesis" and "Techne" in Modern Philosophy and in Aristotle*. South Bend, Indiana: University of Notre Dame Press, 1993.

EDEL, ABRAHAM. *Aristotle and His Philosophy*. Chapel Hill: University of North Carolina Press, 1982.

HUTCHINSON, D. S. "Ethics" in *The Cambridge Companion to Aristotle*. ed. Jonathan Barnes. Cambridge, Cambridge University Press, 1995.

MACINTYRE, ALASDAIR. *After Virtue: A Study in Moral Theory*. South Bend, Indiana: University of Notre Dame Press, 1981.

RORTY, AMELIE OKSENBERG, ed. *Essays on Aristotle's Ethics*. Berkeley: University of California Press, 1980.